We Love Fruit!

By Fay Robinson

Consultants:
Robert L. Hillerich, Ph.D., Bowling Green State University, Bowling Green, Ohio

Mary Nalbandian, Director of Science, Chicago Public Schools, Chicago, Illinois

Design by Beth Herman Design Associates

Library of Congress Cataloging-in-Publication Data

Robinson, Fay.
We love fruit! / by Fay Robinson.
p. cm.
Summary: Discusses different kinds of fruit and how they grow.
ISBN 0-516-06006-6
1. Fruit–Juvenile literature. [1. Fruit.] I. Title.
SB357.2.R63 1992
641.3'4–dc20 92-13312
CIP
AC

Printed in the United States of America.
1 2 3 4 5 6 7 8 9 10 R 00 99 98 97 96 95 94

On a summer day, what do you like to eat? A juicy peach,

a shiny plum,

or maybe a delicious piece of watermelon?

You probably know
that peaches, plums, and
watermelons are all fruits.

So are apples, oranges,
strawberries, grapes, and
bananas. People eat more
bananas than any other
fruit.

Fruits come in many different sizes, shapes, and colors. But there is one thing almost all fruits have in common — seeds.

Sometimes one seed grows in the middle of a fruit.

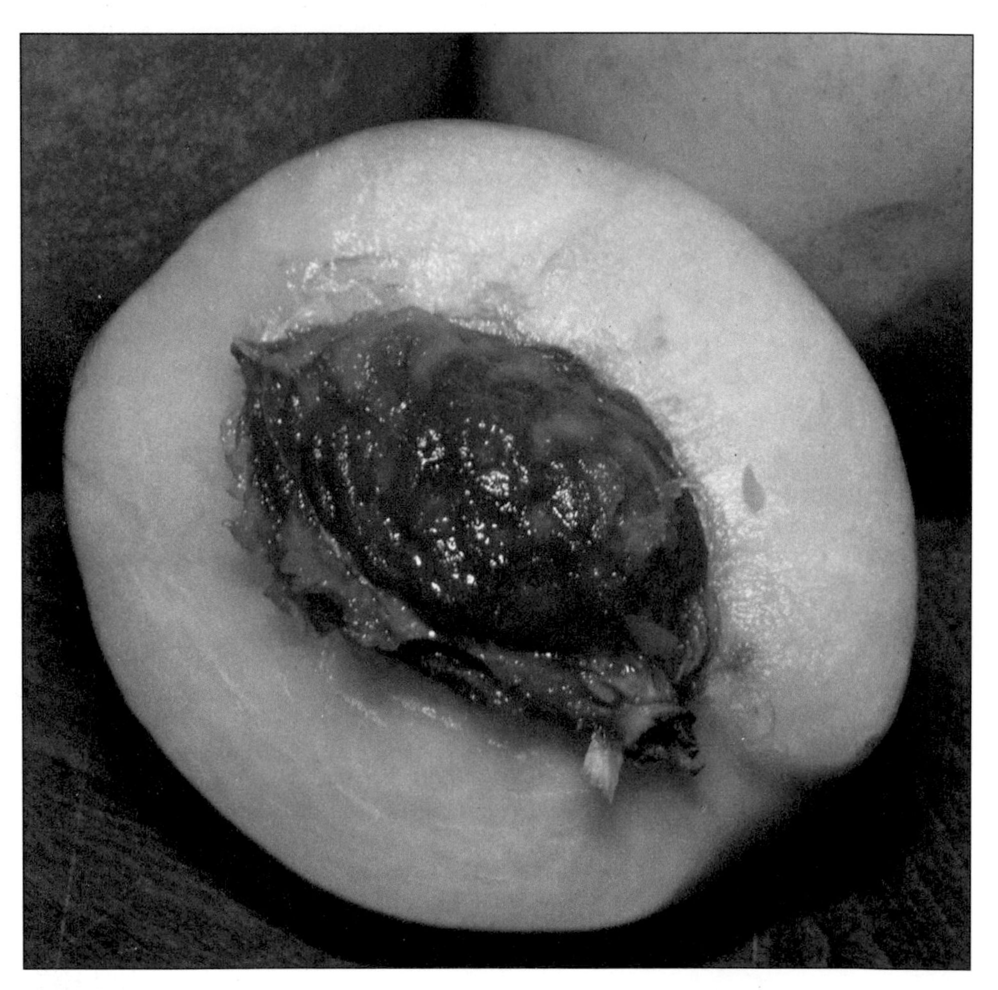

Sometimes a few seeds grow in a star shape.

Sometimes seeds grow in stringy groups.

Sometimes seeds grow all over a fruit.

In nature, the purpose of a fruit is to protect the seeds inside it.

Fruit grows at the base of flowers. Soon the flowers drop off but the fruit keeps growing.

Finally, the fruit falls to the ground. As the fruit rots away, the seeds have a chance to mix with the soil and grow into new plants. The plants use the rotting fruit as food to help them grow.

To a botanist, a scientist who studies plants, a fruit is any covering that grows over seeds. This includes tomatoes, cucumbers, and even acorns.

But most of us think of fruit as the juicy, usually sweet, food we eat.

Fruits grow wild in most parts of the world.

But they're also grown
on farms.

When they are full-grown, fruits are picked, then packed for sale in stores.

SUNKIST NAVEL
ORANGES
79¢ lb
SWEET & CRISPY
JAPANESE
PEAR APPLES
$2.00
EACH
SWEET SEEDLESS
SATSUMA
$1.25
POUND
9.9¢
99¢

Fruits not only taste good,
they are good for you.
They have lots of the
vitamins, minerals, and
natural sugars you need
to stay healthy.

People all over the world eat fruit every day. We love fruit! What's your favorite kind?

Words You Know

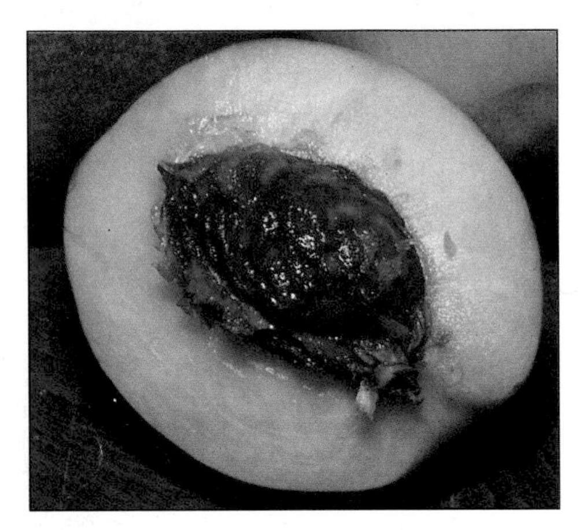

one

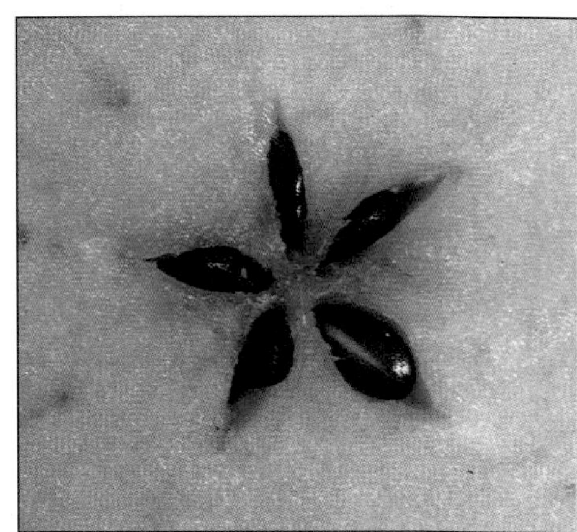

star

seeds

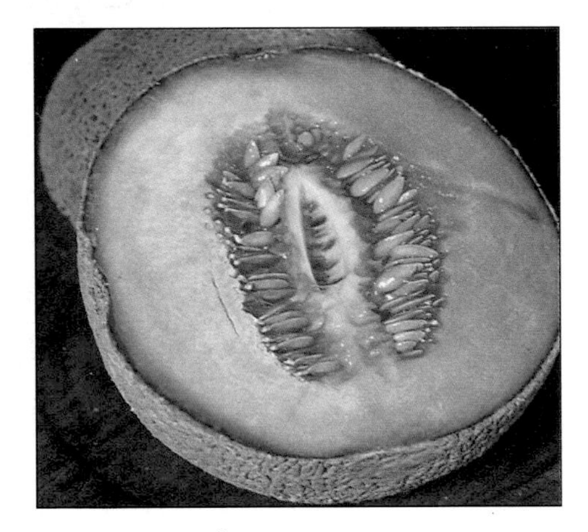

stringy group

all over

peach

plums

watermelon

apples

oranges

strawberries

grapes

bananas

tomato

Index

About the Author

Fay Robinson is an early childhood specialist. She lives and works in the Chicago area.

Photo Credits

PhotoEdit – ©Myrleen Ferguson, 5, 28; ©Tony Freeman, 31 (top right)

Photri – 27

Tom Stack & Associates – ©Terry Donnelly, 25

SuperStock International, Inc. – ©Age Spain, Cover, 31 (center center); ©Lewis Kemper, 15, 31 (bottom left); ©Tom Rosenthal, 22; ©Ping Amranand, 23; ©Sal Maimone, 24

Valan – ©Val & Alan Wilkinson, 3, 14; ©Pam E. Hickman, 4, 31 (top center); ©Joyce Photographics, 6, 31 (bottom center); ©P. A. Wilkinson, 9; ©V. Wilkinson, 10, 11, 12, 30 (top left, top right, bottom left), 31 (top left); ©Michel Bourque, 13, 30 (bottom right), 31 (center right); ©Pierre Kohler, 16; ©J. A. Wilkinson, 17; ©Jeannie R. Kemp, 17 (inset), 31 (center left); ©Kennon Cooke, 19; ©V. Whelan, 20, 31 (bottom right); ©Phillip Norton, 21

COVER: Bowl of fruit